George Hammons' collection *Witness* meditates on the body—its connections to others both human and of the natural world—and our own and others' perceptions of the body, most specifically the black body. Every reader will find something movingly recognizable in these poems. Be sure that you are one of them.

—Lynne Thompson, *Fretwork* and *Beg No Pardon*

George Hammons has a genius for humanity, and these poems help us to gain an understanding of his point of view, and I hope that they have helped me to grow. Certainly, if I haven't, that is my limitation, not his. He is able to see the beauty in a grandmother who cannot say that she loves him, so instead shows it through food, a dead hummingbird, and Jimi Hendrix. He's able to make world events personal and draw us more closely into the tragedies of Trayvon Martin and Robin Williams. This is poetry as it should be, an act of personal spirituality made universal through the expert use of language.

—John Brantingham, Poet Laureate of Sequoia and Kings Canyon National Park

WITNESS: SELECTED POEMS
Copyright © 2020 George Hammons

pictureshowpress.net

Cover Art: Olga_Aleksieieva, istockphoto.com; original hand
            drawn painting for cloth print.

FIRST EDITION

ISBN-13: 978-1-7341702-2-1

Witness

SELECTED POEMS
GEORGE HAMMONS

Picture Show Press

This book is dedicated to my children: Joshua, Jessica and Britany, and to my best bud, Ron King (1955-2018).

POEMS

It's just a cross

until somebody's nailed to it
and then
it's "News!"

A body offered up
sometimes turns a cross
into a crucifix.
Sometimes a body offered up becomes deified; like
Jesus or
Martin or Malcom, like
Amadou or Trayvon,

their bodies broken and evaporating,
their spirits suddenly in flight
become transformed and extolled as if
suddenly within them stand
multitudes
and every *body*
feels the nails.

A Child's Grave

There is a child's grave
in a derelict cemetery in Phoenix, Arizona
with my exact name on the headstone:
George Henry Hammons III.

To make a long story short,
I discovered it by accident,
but I have stood before it many times since.

While there, I sometimes become confused,
I imagine that it is my grave;
standing there, I sometimes think
if we dug up this grave
and unearthed the body,
it would be mine.

I don't know if it would rise up
in a dreadful scream
or if it would cause *me* to simply burst into dust,
but I truly believe that something powerful would ensue
and join me to a
dead child's *self:*
like two halves
becoming something frighteningly complete.

I sometimes consider
perhaps
it is just my dreams
buried here
along with my aspirations;

dead potential lain to rest
before it was ever born,
signified by this gravestone,

with *my* name

and yet again there are moments in which I believe
perhaps my fears
are buried here,
perhaps
my disappointments and my shortcomings.
Perhaps it is my sorrows,
happy to have found a place
other than my heart
to call home.

I always bring a cloth and soap and water
to wash the headstone.
I leave fresh flowers,
but I know that they will soon be dead as well;
because in this merciless heat,
cut flowers
like prayers,
quickly whither away.

I ponder that no other loving hands
have been here
since *my* last visit,
no one else seems to care that the birds and dirt
reflect so poorly on this grave
so I care
that this task is done,
so I care
that this child with my name
lived and died.

And so, if soap and water and a moment's penance
in this hellish heat
can allay a dead child's secluded spirit,
even if only for a moment

then *I care*
and I am grateful
to wash this stone that weighs on me
and preoccupies my mind.
I happily wash the dirt
from my own name
because for a moment as the gray granite comes clean
I suddenly know that
I am alive.

Suddenly, as my hand passes over each letter, I know
that this child was someone else
and I realize that it doesn't matter
if it is hope or regret
that is buried here

because neither one will amount to more
than *this* moment's meditation
of soap and water,

but as quickly as it was won,
my little victory of self-confidence is gone
and I am once again *the name*
that is written on this headstone
and I am once again
fearfully haunting a child's grave
in a derelict cemetery
in Phoenix, Arizona;
Because no one else will.

The loss of a child

for Sybrina Fulton, Tracy Martin and Trayvon

At the news of your death
the earth buckled and threw me into the air.
From here the only thing I know is that
there will not be a soft landing.

I feel as if all the breath has been driven from my body.
I cannot talk, or scream, or cry.
I feel as if my clothes are on fire.
I am burning like an object
entering earth's atmosphere.

From here looking down
nothing is familiar;
there are no landmarks,
there is nothing to recognize or understand.

From here looking down
there are only the thousand things
I would have said
had I known
I would never see you alive again.
I would have said a thousand things
just to say, this one: *I love you*
more than money, more than religion, more than myself.
I love *you*.

I wish that in the end
I had said something *especially* nice, shared a hug
or a kiss, a moment to look in your young eyes,
a smile.
But I didn't know that I would never see you, alive again.

Oh, I am not flying,

I am flung
and when I again touch earth
I may shatter like glass.

From here, the only thing that I *know* is
that there will not be a soft landing.

The Siren

there is a siren in my poem
but I am not afraid
it's not for me
it screams
someone else's name
like notes blared from the
inside of a
jazz riff
or like the din of
an explosion
and the deafness which immediately follows
like the burbled wail of a mother's grief
its yowl the
nonstop crimson
in its attenuation
in its resolve
it tumbles
thick as honey
dense as guilt
as it slow motion spills
its
syrupy red
howl
into our ears and down the street

Babylon

for everybody from Compton

Night falls on Babylon
and her favorite son
gently covers the old whore
with a blanket,
a blanket
woven from the despair of thousands of innocents.

The boy gently kisses the old bitch's evil face
and for a moment he sees the beginnings of a smile
on her cruel lips.

The boy smiles and quietly returns to the table,
where she has, as she does every night,
drank herself to sleep.

He clears away the dirty dishes,
shakes the crumbs from the tablecloth
and then stares at the stars out the window
over the kitchen sink.

Mrs. Balis

for Anthony P. Davis

was an ugly woman
or at least as a child I thought her ugly.
She tolerated me,
the desperate black kid
who couldn't remember numbers,
but had a mouth,
could argue the time of day,
uppity little nigger
coming to class looking grubby,
she not knowing that I might have spent the night
hunched against a tin shed and I never told anyone
because
kids fear embarrassment more than death;
and daddy drunk and *toting*
and who would we call anyway?
And so my sisters and I evacuated
and survived
so that Mrs. Balis could call me to her desk to tell
me I didn't write the poem
I turned in for English and she could look
smugly as if she had apprehended some great
literary fraud
until
my best friend Tony laughed and snorted something
like, "Yes, he did! George writes poems all of the time."
And Mrs. Balis squeezes out a tiny gasp because
now she suddenly sees
a fucking unicorn.

Home

I think about our disjointed
almost acrobatic existence,
and one night in particular,
us poised
upon
a rickety wooden bench,
huddled like baby birds,
me reaching down in the dark to pluck
a blade of sanity
from the un-mowed chaos
where I had always thought nothing could hurt "Me."
But now
we are all hair's breaths, whispering
into a calamity, our voices becoming
flecks of stones,
rust and smoke;
2:30 am and us with school tomorrow
7 or 8 years old
and sleepless.

Something frightening is in our house,
a ranging disaster
like a big dangerous cat, or a time bomb
or a ghost;
our youth devoured
in angry, intoxicating gulps
and we will never know the truth
of why
except that it has left us unable to embrace
one another
as if
to do so would awaken
what it was that we so astutely learned to fear.

All of the things we broke

come back in pieces
to haunt us,
little hands and little feet,
little fists and little teeth;
pray for hands to war
and fingers to fight
so that in the dark
we pray for sight
and forgiveness,
though
it is slow
in coming.

Doves

My daughter calls me to the balcony;
pointing to the tree beyond, she says, "Look,
doves have built a nest
and there is a chick."

The instant I look,
a hawk pounces down, through the branches,
and methodically claws the nest apart,
it then leaps away with the chick in its beak.

The expression on my daughter's face is something blessed,
a poignant grace visits her; and a visual prayer
of brown eyes and surprise says that somehow
she knows about hawks and doves, and so she does not judge.

We exchange an instant of amazement that such a thing
could happen at just this moment;
Secretly,
I wonder if it was somehow our gaze that gave
the nest's location away. I am hurt,
guilty of being a witness.
From time to time, for the next few days, I see
the confused parent-doves light
on nearby branches and survey their tattered nest,
or they strut on the patio railing and coo.

And something for the ants

I passed a dead hummingbird lying right
in the middle of a busy walkway.
I was a step past it when I realized that it wasn't a leaf;
I went back and looking down, I realized
I had never seen a dead hummingbird before.
I've seen them darting here and there,
drawing nectar. I've seen their little nests
with tiny eggs,
I've seen them light for a moment upon a branch or
just hover inquisitively in front of me in midair,
all shiny and sprite-like,
but I had never seen one dead.
It was momentarily startling
like stumbling upon a dead unicorn.

Its beak open, as if to speak,
its one exposed eye, a tiny dark pit, like a miniature
black hole, suddenly centering my universe,
its gravity, unavoidable,
pulled me into a sorrow, where suddenly
everyone whom I've ever lost stared out at me
as if daring me to appreciate the idea of
this single hummingbird's importance,

its bright feathers *blunted,* as death is wont to do,
in taking the sheen from living things
and suddenly this is so *real*
all of the magic that was once a hummingbird is gone
and in its place, a tiny trampled shell.

My neighbor's chubby yellow cat
lies twenty feet away, grooming himself,
unconcerned,
feigning nonchalance

and even though I have no evidence, I suspect him
but what cunning, what magic
could he conjure up that he could kill a
hummingbird.

Unsure of what else to do,
I walk on,
but it gets to me:
The bird; dead, there in the walkway, its beak open
as if to speak, its tiny eye a dark universe pulling at
me, its dull feathers, and the heartbreak of it all
so I go back with a baggie,
I scoop it up (surprised at the heft for such a little thing),

I take it to the hedge wall, and
lay it there, where it is quiet and cool,
and something for the ants.

Today's beachcombing is done

I think I'll go down to the shore,
see what the tide's brought in.
I love to walk the beach
and watch the day begin.
Sometimes I find a thing or two
to place upon my shelf:
a shell, a piece of driftwood,
sea stars, or something else,
perhaps a bottled message
or something that is rare.
It really doesn't matter
as long as the weather's fair.

But when I get there,
"Not today,"
 says my policeman friend.
"Haitians, crazy Haitians"
are what the tides brought in
on homemade boats they set afloat
to try the dire straits,
on homemade boats they've placed their hopes.
Now on the beach they wait.
Bodies, so many bodies have washed up on the sand,
like sleepers who lie napping.
The bodies stretch along the strand.
I realize the irony;
their destination's reached,
and Haitians, crazy Haitians
lie waiting on the beach.
I watch as they are gathered
and carried one by one,
until the beach is cleared
and today's beachcombing is done.

For the hundreds of Haitians who perished during what is called "the boat crisis" and for the thousands of people here in the U.S. and around the world who suffer as refugees.

James Blake: Got Tackled

"If you have never struggled with someone who is resisting arrest or who pulled a gun or knife on you when you approached them for breaking a law, then you are not qualified to judge the actions of police officers putting themselves in harm's way for the public good.

"It is mystifying to all police officers to see pundits and editorial writers whose only expertise is writing fast-breaking, personal opinion, and who have never faced the dangers that police officers routinely do, come to instant conclusions that an officer's actions were wrong based upon nothing but a silent video. That is irresponsible, unjust and un-American."

— A spokesperson for the Patrolmen's Benevolent Association, New York City police union, September 2015

If you have never been Black
and looked in the rearview mirror when you're driving
and seen a police car
and been afraid, even though you were doing nothing wrong,
then you are not qualified to judge.

If you have never been Black
and had a police car pass you
while you were walking on the street
and had that cop make eye contact
and you became afraid for your personal safety
even though you were not doing anything wrong,
then you are not qualified to judge.

If you have never been Black
and had to protest to get the same accommodations
that white people take for granted
even though you are willing to pay for them,

then you are not qualified to judge.

If you have never been Black
and faced fire hoses and police dogs
and billy clubs and jail
just so you could vote, or go to school,
or hold a civil servants' job,
then you are not qualified to judge.

If you have never been Black
and worked from *caint' see* to *caint'* see
for table scraps, and no money
and the opportunity to sleep on the ground,
then you are not qualified to judge.

If you have never been Black
and put on your best clothes
and rode up to the big house
and sat there mounted
with your six shooter
and your pride
only to have old ugly Stephen
come limpin' out at Candyland
asking,
"Who dis niggah on that nag?"
then you are not qualified to judge.

If you have never been Black
and stripped naked, and been poked
and prodded, and pinched, had your mouth
held open, so that potential buyers could examine your teeth,
if you have never been Black
and sold, away from your family and friends,
then you are not qualified to judge.

Black Words on White Paper

What difference in our world would we see
if ink were white and paper black;

would literature, religion, history, philosophy,
(you or me)
say something more relevant, more observant?

Or would our words simply bleed
an amalgam of pulp and dye; gray have true
characters with faint edges
that tire the eye and lull readers to sleep?

Black paper, white ink; what if all the news and
everything we think
were brought to us that way?

Would we then have sayings like, *It was a white day*,
meaning dirty, soiled, disastrous, diabolic or immoral?

Would we then say "black" when we wanted to portray
clean, pure, heroic, true or honorable?

I come from a world of white paper and black ink,
but still I like to waste my time and think;
what if it were the other way 'round?

What Work You Can Get

You can't know where you're going
if you don't know where you've been
There is a nice sentiment to these words
but in the noonday sun
with hard work to be done
where I've been
is of no help
My granddaddy
and my daddy
are of no help
They left me no
"Old money"
No grub steak
No future
My granny and my mammy
are of no help
even though their hearts are as solid
as this ground
and their affections
are as unwavering
as that tree stump yonder
Where I've been is of little consequence
Where I *am* is digging stumps
for an old white man
who sits sipping
whiskey and water
in the shade
of an old oak tree
which he will soon order me
to chop down

Funnymen

for Robin

It's all laughs until somebody hangs themself.

Funnymen are falling from the sky, laughing,
their faces contorted by the rush of air
across their bleached teeth.
Some are falling head first,
others pose almost gracefully
as if they are descending
Gods.

I am on the ground,
astonished
because just at the moment when their impact seems
imminent, they stall
and are pulled back up as if yo-yoed by an unseen hand
only to be hurled down again,
their hurtling bodies laughing, their haggard
clothes crackling,
their skin blistered and almost alight from the friction
while their jokes
fall like blood spatter across all of us
who lack a *real* sense of humor.

Jimi
(Hendrix of course)

Like a photographer's flash
going off too close to our eyes,
the brilliance disrupted by blindness
then everything coming back into focus,
the whir of colors; black blues, fire reds,
and him standing above us:
a gunslinger,
a pirate,
a peacock
calling out
"Look at the sky
        turn hell fire red, y'all."
Our minds alight
as we become
the blues,
charged and rough,
no longer just the aimless topography of a small
town,
no longer just the lover or the yearning,
but the world burning
in our imaginations
and he lights his ax on fire,
sacrificed,
hissing like a jet
where in his wake
we dance.

The Anthem

We have our own, you know? James Weldon Johnson's 1900 poem
implored us to *Lift Every Voice*. His brother, as brothers will do,
looking for something to disrupt, said "Ah, music!" and so John
Rosamond Johnson in 1905 set the poem to music, and so we sang,
"Lift every voice and sing, till earth and heaven ring." So much
kinder than "no refuge could save the hireling and slave."
But that's just me.

My Grandmother's Kitchen

smelled of coffee and bacon and biscuits.
It didn't smell like that every day,
but that's the smell I always associate with the place
(and she did love some breakfast).
She was born in the early 1900s and for a mulatto girl
(White Irish father, Black mother), in Natchez, Mississippi,
education consisted of
homemaking and housekeeping;
cookn' and cleaning.

Our table at Thanksgiving was impeccable.
It was the physical memory of her finishing-school
experience;
everything she knew about etiquette manifested
on that table.
All of the "Good stuff" on display; each item
in its proper place,
polished silverware, gold-rimmed glasses,
seldom-used platters and
plates. Everything poised as if in anticipation
of that delicious turkey and dressing, sweet pickles
and cranberries, candied yams, biscuits and butter, ice tea
and lemonade, peach cobblers
and homemade ice cream.
We were poor people, but I swear
you couldn't tell it on Thanksgiving.

I think that the only good furniture in my
grandmother's house was in the dining room:
big, heavy, claw-footed stuff,
dark and serious;
most of the year it served as a place that I hid
under, playing with little Hot Wheels cars and army men.
Sometimes it served as the work surface for school

projects and homework.
Oh, but sometimes that old sleepy table *woke up*
and was transformed into crystal and silver,
shining from stem to stern.

On regular days, we had spaghetti, and chicken
wings, chili and stew; my grandmother would
sometimes
get recipes from cereal boxes or magazines
and she was never afraid to experiment thus my love of tuna
and cornflake casseroles, canned fruit embedded in Jello,
sock-it-to me and seven-up cakes, fried pies
filled with jelly. On regular days, we sat at the little green
Formica table in the kitchen and took our meals.

I guess what I'm really trying to tell you is that
in my grandmother's house,
food was the medium through which she created
edible still lifes,
performance art
which we gladly gobbled up.

My grandmother was never the type to just come
out and say, "I love you."
I doubt that anyone had said that to her
in such a long time
and so (I think) she poured what love she had
into our meals.

I can remember her standing back, doing final
inspections over her holiday table, one
hand pensively posed by her face as if asking
herself what she might have forgotten, and
I'm sure that the answer was always "nothing," but
she'd ask herself anyway.

I wish that her story had a happy ending because

ultimately it was food that killed her;
too much sugar, too much salt and fat, too many
pieces of fried chicken and pork chops, potatoes and rice,
just too much.
Diabetes and heart disease took their toll
and in the end she had to give up all of that food
she loved,
all of the food that she taught us to love.

My grandmother's kitchen was a tiny space,
where I learned how to cook,
where I learned how to say *I love you*
without actually having to say it;
in hindsight,
where the alchemy of infusing food with love
was practiced
and where, in hindsight, in a roundabout way,
through my grandmother's example,
I learned how to eat to live.

Two days after a heart attack

I think that it is my grandmother's voice, I think that she is in the
  kitchen cooking.
I hear pots and pans and women laughing and for some reason I
  think that it is *Thanksgiving*.
I think that I am in the old house, but my eyes are closed and I
  don't want to open them for fear of breaking the spell.

I can hear my wife's voice and my daughters are there, my sisters
  are there, too.
It is as if every woman I have ever loved is just beyond that door.

Shhh someone is talking about me by name, and I can't make out
  the words,
but they are speaking *kindly* and everyone is agreeing until…

Ohhhh shit, it's 6:00 a.m. and the nurse is here, she wants my
  blood, and says, "Just a little stick," and with that, and a
  quick-dimpled smile, she has what she came for, and is gone.

Gone, too, are my dreams of *Thanksgiving*. The voices beyond the
  door are now low and practiced and unfamiliar, their tones
  matter of fact, the pots and pans have turned to clipboards
  and wheels rolling in the hallway.

And I am left smiling inside of this pain that is my aching heart.

Some horses

are simply meant to plow straight ahead. They don't zig or zag, they are not inquisitive, they consider it *exciting* to reach the end of a furrow and make a U-turn. They do not like, or dislike, the controlling hands at the other end of their reigns; they are simply familiar. Some horses could almost complete the tilling alone, without the snap of straps, or the mouth clicks, or the *attaboys*, the *whoas, or ghee-up those U-turns,* where the plowshare is lifted then dropped again at precisely the right moment would be "tricky" and so maybe some horses would simply never turn, destined to be stymied by a fence or an obstacle somewhere down the line, or their furrows might curve back, one upon the other, like an abstract work of art which they could never appreciate from their grounded level. Some horses are meant to live out their lives blinded; that behind them, the earth is giving way, cleaved in a promise of growth that they will never conceive as important, or necessary, or even as the result of their efforts. They may from time to time look upon a neighboring field where crops are near maturity, and smile to themselves, *"Soon I will get to pull the wagon."*

Purgatory

I am sitting in a tea shop that glistens white subways,
I am surrounded by students who stare intently at their Macs or
    iPhones.
Everyone looks like models,
their clothes distressingly expensive,
their hair, too, cut and dyed so that even as they
lean over it falls *just so.*
I am fascinated that the cash registers (for lack
of a better term) look like iPads;
the girl behind the counter smiles, as students tip
their phones against a scanner and "ping!" success, tea!
The staff behind the counter wear white shirts
with blue pinstripes,
they are *so* "cute."
My date beams sunshine, straight into me,
across a waffle disguised as dessert,
and a leafy drink that makes me grateful for coffee.
And somewhere in my wonderment I ask,
Is this is 'purgatory'?
A brief respite from the hell outside?
Something to cherish?
This moment for my date's sunshine,
the "cute" staff,
the iPads, the "ping!"
the tea,
the distressingly expensive clothes and haircuts,
the students who look like models,
the Macs and iPhones,
the white glistening subways.
As soon as we leave,
someone runs the red light just at the corner
and as we skid around each other, in the rain, almost close
enough to kiss, I see the other driver, eyes like
teacups. And all that I can seem to say is,
"Awwww Hell."

Wonder Woman

The way that sunlight delights in the fine hairs on
the side of your face
the way that *one* eyebrow arcs
in communion with a skeptic's pursing
and the slightest tilt of your head
the holiness in your humming
the way you drive
Fast
your eyes
by candlelight
and me talking and talking
until your hand is holding mine
and the quiet
says everything that I could not
the way you lean into me when we walk
the way you smell
the way you taste
the way that you read my body with your hands
like brail
the way at two o'clock in the morning
you are not tired of me
the way that you understand my dreams
the way that you wrap around me
and melt
and melt
and melt

She says, "Merry fuckin Christmas

Now take your shit and go." And she slams the door.

So...
I am now standing outside,

the weight of so many botched
moments seems to have accumulated
and I am now holding them
just behind my eyes

where they wait,
like prisoners
who have idly watched opportunity pass them by.

And this is California, so it's 80 degrees
and I'm sweating
and this is California and so Jesus (who lives
just down the street), blond and tan
with six pack abs (which are somehow always on display),
skate boards over,
and with a twinkle in his eye,
he says,
"Dang, bro, that's tough.
And she's really cute for an older lady."

Oh, I could punch him in his perfect fuckn' teeth,
but I am fickle
about Jesus, and love and Christmas

and the fact that every day might have been a gift,
an opportunity
to realize that miracles reside inside of human beings.
I might have *celebrated* these everyday gifts
a little bit more,

like the first time that I saw sunlight display
the true color in my lover's eyes, and I didn't say
anything, I just looked. Her eyes are beautiful,
I should have told her.
Or all of the times that I heard the sound
of her voice, sensual and quiet and intimately close,
and I did not rejoice,
or just the fact she was ok with *giving* and *taking,*
she *tried* (and I mean that in a good way).
The thousand chances to say something nice,
and maybe I was afraid to appear corny or weak.
Anyway, all of those moments are moments which I will
never have back.
Could have made for her a Christmas of every day,
Oh! But I'm standing outside sweating, thinking
to myself (because Jesus is long gone),
Fucking Christmas.

How to make a bed by yourself

First pull off the old bedding: the comforter,
the blanket, the top sheet, the fitted sheet. See what is
there left? A stark mattress. Allow yourself a
moment to appreciate any signs of wear. Perhaps a
lonely dip impresses one side as if to show how you
have favored being curled there. If need be, rotate or
flip your mattress (as if something about this act
will make everything come out fair). Now take your
fresh linen and spread the fitted bottom sheet with
the reverence of a prayer. Tuck the rounded ends
home when the bottom sheet is in place, guide your
palms smoothly across any wrinkles, and see how
this foundation like a blank canvas has suddenly
become hopeful. Take the top sheet and, standing at
the bottom of the bed, snap it forward, holding your
arms outstretched so that it unfurls and floats down
like a dream while your hands drift gently, like a
symphony conductor's, to a surface that you tuck and
smooth as if it is new skin. Return the blanket and
the comforter, place fresh pillow cases, and return
the pillows to their rest. Finally, appreciate and, once
again, smooth everything under your hopeful palms.

El Gato Grande

I am driving slow;
it is just dusk enough for lights.
The grade slopes up slightly
and *now* against the red and gold horizon,
a shape steps from the median.
At first, I think it is a man,
bent on all fours,
but then he turns his big square head towards me
and without rising,
strolls,
deliberate as winter,
across the street,
pauses
at the opposing slope,
narrows his eyes at my headlights
and leaps,
light as a saint
into the darkness.

ACKNOWLEDGEMENTS

Thank you Shannon Phillips (my publisher) for your courage and kindness and for always saying "I got this." Jennifer Chen (Yoga and Meditation instructor) for helping me to understand that in this body I'm not just a passenger, but I am also a navigator and a pilot. For my teachers, Chad Sweeney and Juan Delgado, whose voices I hear constantly as I edit. And for the MFA and undergrad students at CSUSB who are too numerous to name, but who are near and dear to me (you know who you are).

www.ingramcontent.com/pod-product-compliance
Lightning Source LLC
Chambersburg PA
CBHW021148020426
42331CB00005B/948